# cool smoothies

### juices and cocktails

# cool smoothies
## juices and cocktails

elsa petersen-schepelern

**photography by** james merrell,
william lingwood and debi treloar

RYLAND
PETERS
& SMALL

London  New York

**Designer** Emilie Ekström
**Editor** Miriam Hyslop
**Production** Meryl Silbert
**Art Director** Gabriella Le Grazie
**Publishing Director** Alison Starling

**Food Stylists** Elsa Petersen-Schepelern,
Bridget Sargeson, David Peacock
**Stylists** Wei Tang, Helen Trent

First published in the United Kingdom in 2002
by Ryland Peters & Small
Kirkman House
12–14 Whitfield Street
London W1T 2RP

ISBN 1 84172 281 2

**Author's Acknowledgements**
My heartfelt thanks to James Merrell, William Lingwood
and Debi Treloar for their beautiful photographs, to Wei
Tang and Helen Trent for delightful props, and to two of
my favourite designers, Emilie Ekström and Louise Leffler,
for making me look good. Thanks also to my family,
Kirsten Bray, Peter Bray and Nowelle Valentino-Capezza,
and to friends who helped imbibe these goodies, Tim,
Tessa, Martin, Susan, Sheridan, Mike and Karen.

# contents

# a cool smooth summer

Drinks in the garden, lunch on the deck, barbecues, tennis parties and sunbathing – all essential summer pastimes requiring the drinks in this book. You'll find recipes for children and adults, drinks with and without alcohol, cocktails for one, or party drinks for many. Almost all include fruit and vegetables and are an easy, delicious way to imbibe your vitamins.

# fruits of the earth

Fruit smoothies, juices and shakes — what better ways can there be to have the five daily servings of fruit and vegetables that doctors recommend for good health? All you need is a blender — a hand-held stick blender will do — or a juicing machine if you're very lucky, and this healthy, delicious collection of fruit drinks is within your grasp.

# strawberry
## ice cream
## smoothie

Strawberry smoothies are invariably the most popular with guests – and with me! Serve them made just with ice, or with yoghurt (to make a lassi), ice cream or milk. Or with the lot. Self-indulgence is a very good thing, in my view.

A variation on this recipe doesn't even need a blender – make a Strawberry Spider in a tall glass with a scoop of strawberry ice cream, 1 tablespoon liqueur or strawberry syrup, then top up with soda (preferably strawberry). Pour in the soda very carefully: it fizzes like mad!

*12 ice cubes*
*4 scoops strawberry ice cream*
*12 large, ripe strawberries, hulled and halved*
*125 ml plain low-fat yoghurt, or to taste*
*low-fat milk, to taste*
**SERVES 1–2**

Put the ice cubes into a blender and blend to a snow. Add the ice cream, strawberries and yoghurt and blend again, adding just enough milk to let the blades run. Pour into glasses and serve.

**VARIATION** Add extra ice cream for a thicker smoothie, or extra milk, to taste. Serve with an extra small scoop of ice cream balanced on the edge of the glass (if possible).

# fruit salad lassi
## with
## strawberries

Lassi is the famous Indian drink made with yoghurt and ice, thinned down with a little water. It is served either salty or sweet, flavoured with fruit, nuts or spices. It is very cool and refreshing on a hot summer's day.

Strawberries, mangoes, papayas or bananas are perfect fruits to team up with milk and yoghurt.

Yoghurt is a great source of calcium, especially for women – use the low-fat kind if you're watching your waistline.

*250 ml low-fat plain yoghurt*
*125 ml low-fat milk*
*6 large strawberries, hulled and halved*
*a choice of other fruit, such as 1 small punnet*
   *raspberries, 6 apricots or 2 peaches, pitted*
*sugar, to taste*
*crushed ice, to serve*
**SERVES 2–4**

Put the yoghurt, milk, strawberries and other fruit into a blender and process until creamy. Add sugar to taste and serve poured over crushed ice.

**VARIATION** Instead of the fruit listed, use the pulp and seeds of 4 passionfruit, plus 1 tablespoon Galliano or Grand Marnier liqueur.

# strawberry juice
## with balsamic

Balsamic – the rich, slightly sweet, aged
vinegar from Italy – should be used in
moderation: use it like a spice, don't slap
it on like ordinary vinegar. It also has an
extraordinary affinity with strawberries.
Rinse the berries before hulling, or they
will fill with water.

*2 punnets ripe strawberries*
*1 tablespoon honey (optional)*
*6 ice cubes*
*balsamic vinegar*
**SERVES 2–4**

Reserve a few strawberries for decoration, then
put the remainder into a blender with the honey,
if using, and the ice cubes. Blend well, adding
water if necessary to make the mixture easier to
work. Blend again, then serve in a tiny shot glass,
over ice, with a halved strawberry on top. Serve
the balsamic separately, in drops.

Strawberries with balsamic vinegar – it sounds a rather odd combination, but balsamic acts like lemon juice, to point up other flavours, and its sweet, spicy undertones have an extraordinarily delicious effect. Vinegar also acts as an aid to digestion, prevents fatigue and lessens the risk of high blood pressure.

## pineapple and
# strawberry crush

A summer cooler that's simply the most glorious colour and tastes like heaven!

*1 medium pineapple, peeled and cored*
*10–12 ripe strawberries*
*grated zest and juice of 2 lemons*
*2 tablespoons icing sugar, or to taste*
*juice of 2 oranges*

**to serve**
*ice cubes or crushed ice*
*3–6 strawberries, sliced*
*a twist of orange, lime or lemon zest*
**SERVES 6–8**

Put the pineapple, strawberries, lemon zest and icing sugar into a blender, add about 125 ml iced water and purée until smooth. Add the orange and lemon juices and another 125 ml iced water. Taste and add extra sugar if necessary (depending on the sweetness of the fruit). Pour into a jug of ice and decorate with sliced berries and a twist of orange or lemon peel.

## rhubarb
# strawberryade

This unusual, old-fashioned drink is based on homemade lemonade. Make it with pretty pink forced rhubarb for an utterly stunning colour, or add a dash of Grenadine to point up the pink.

*500 g rhubarb, trimmed and sliced*
*2 tablespoons icing sugar*
*grated zest and juice of 1 lemon*
*6 strawberries, hulled and halved*

**to serve**
*ice cubes or crushed ice*
*sparkling mineral water*
**SERVES 4–8**

Put the rhubarb, sugar and lemon zest into a saucepan and cover with at least 1 litre boiling water. Stew until the rhubarb is very soft. Add the strawberries and boil hard for about 1 minute, then strain into a jug, cool and chill. To serve, pour into a jug of ice, stir in the lemon juice and top up with sparkling mineral water.

Strawberries in any guise please the palate and look wonderfully pretty. They're terrific with pineapple and sensational with rhubarb.

*1 ripe peach, peeled and halved*

*1 ripe nectarine, halved*

*2 ripe apricots, halved*

*a handful of raspberries*

*6 ice cubes*

*sparkling mineral water, to taste*

*honey or sugar (optional)*

**SERVES 2**

Discard the stones from the fruit. Put all the fruit into a blender, add the ice and enough mineral water to make the blades run. Blend to a purée.

Add honey or sugar to taste, then enough extra water to produce the consistency you like. Pour into glasses and serve.

# summer fruit crush
## with peach,
## nectarine, apricots
## and raspberries

In summer, when fruit is good quality, plentiful and relatively inexpensive, make this fruity mixture in bigger quantities for a party. Take care with your choice of fruit though – keep it red, orange and yellow – if you add green fruits, such as kiwifruit, you'll spoil the colour. Blend the fruit with ice to break up the fibres and help extract all the juice.

I like it made with mineral water, but you could use cherryade for a children's party. If the fruit is sweet and ripe you may not need any sugar or honey.

Most berries are better blended rather than juiced and are delicious mixed with other fruits. They are also good mixed with yoghurt in smoothies and lassis. (In fact, plain low-fat yoghurt is the best form of calcium for women and will help soothe your digestion.)

# berry ice blocks
## with buttermilk
# froth

Freeze a selection of fresh juices in an ice cube tray and serve with buttermilk for a delicious breakfast on a hot day. These ice cubes have been made with cranberry juice and strawberry purée.

*1 tray of ice cubes made with fruit juices*
*500 ml buttermilk or low-fat yoghurt*
*sparkling mineral water or soda water (optional)*
*honey, to taste*

**SERVES 4**

Fill 4 glasses with the fruity ice cubes, add a dollop of buttermilk or yoghurt, then top with sparkling mineral water or soda water, if using. Serve honey separately and add to taste.

The ice cubes melt slowly into the drink, so you can top it up with more buttermilk or more mineral water for a long, cool, delicious and filling drink.

Modern buttermilks are simply skimmed milks blended with a light culture, similar to yoghurt. Serve poured over frozen fruit juices. Ice cubes made from fruit juice melt more slowly than ordinary cubes – so they're good for a long, leisurely breakfast (and kids love them too!)

# cranberry
## cooler

Cranberry mixed with citrus juice is a marriage made in heaven – the prettiest, cloudy pink. The most famous is, of course, the Sea Breeze, but if you're aiming for a healthful drink early in the day, rather than at the cocktail hour, this cooler is for you. Supermarkets sell many versions of cranberry juice, both sweetened and unsweetened. I prefer it unsweetened, but please yourself.

*crushed ice*
*250 ml cranberry juice*
*250 ml orange juice*

**to serve**
*sparkling mineral water*
*a twist of orange peel*
**SERVES 1–2**

Fill a jug with ice, pour over the cranberry and orange juice and stir well. Top up with sparkling water and serve with a twist of orange peel.

Whole cranberries are usually cooked, because they are very tart indeed. The juice is available sweetened or unsweetened, so choose one to suit your taste. Cranberries are high in vitamin C and antioxidants, which protect against cancer and heart disease and help ease the pain of arthritis.

A daily helping of blueberries contains enough antioxidants to improve balance, coordination and short-term memory.

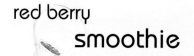

# red berry
## smoothie

Even people with dairy intolerance are often able to eat yoghurt, since it changes its structure during fermentation. It's marvellous for upset stomachs too!

*1 punnet berries (about 250 g), such as*
*strawberries, cranberries, redcurrants or*
*raspberries (for a pink smoothie) or blackberries*
*and blueberries (for a blue smoothie)*
*250 ml plain yoghurt*
*125 ml crushed ice*
*sugar or honey, to taste*

**SERVES 2–3**

Put all the ingredients into a blender and work to a thin, frothy cream. If too thick, add water to create a pourable consistency.

Taste, then add sugar or honey if you prefer.

Vitamin C is vital for life and fresh fruit and juice is the best way of getting it. Commercial juices are often pasteurized or heat-treated to sterilize and preserve them. Heat destroys vitamin C, so manufacturers replace it in the form of ascorbic acid. Remember, real fruit contains real vitamins.

## blueberry and
# orange smoothie

*freshly squeezed juice of 4 oranges*
*1 punnet blueberries, about 250 g*
*sugar (optional)*

**SERVES 1–2**

Put the orange juice into a blender, add the blueberries and blend until smooth. Add sugar to taste, if using.

Alternatively, I often peel the oranges, then feed half of them through a juicer, followed by the blueberries, then the remaining oranges.

# berry, apricot and
## orange slush

Orange juice will help to extend more
expensive fruits, and their gentle acidity
also develops the flavour. Apricots are
very dense, so you may like to pulp them
in the blender rather than putting them
through the juicer. If you do decide to
juice, remove the skins first, and juice
them alternately with pieces of apple.

*8 ripe apricots, halved and pitted,*
   *then coarsely chopped*
*8 strawberries, hulled and halved*
*juice of 2 oranges*
**SERVES 1**

Put the apricots, strawberries and orange juice
into a blender and purée until smooth, adding
water if needed. (If the mixture is too thick, add a
few ice cubes and blend again.)

**Note**  To remove the apricot skins, bring a
saucepan of water to the boil, then blanch the
apricots for about 1 minute. Remove the skin with
the back of a knife.

## granny's
# orangeade

My grandmother was rather good at cooking – a talent she passed on to my mother. I found this deliciously orangy recipe scribbled in one of her falling-apart, yellowing cookbooks.

*4 oranges*
*1 tablespoon sugar, or to taste*
*freshly squeezed juice of 1 lemon*
*ice, to serve*
**SERVES 2–4**

Peel the zest from the oranges, leaving the white pith behind. Put the zest into a jug with the sugar, then add the orange and lemon juice. Pour over 1 litre boiling water, let stand until cool, strain and serve over ice.

## old-fashioned
# orangeade

These old-fashioned drinks are not fizzy like modern soft drinks. For fizz, make a stronger mixture by decreasing the quantity of water, then serve the drinks topped up with sparkling mineral water or soda. I added fizz by serving through a Sodastream® machine.

*2 oranges, sliced and deseeded, but unpeeled*
*1 lemon, sliced and deseeded, but unpeeled*
*50 g sugar, or to taste*
*a curl of orange zest, to serve*
**SERVES 2–4**

Put the sliced oranges, lemon and sugar into a large jug, pour over 1–1.25 litres boiling water, cover, cool and chill. Serve, strained over glasses of ice, with a curl of orange zest.

Alternatively, double the quantity of fruit, peel the zest, discarding any white pith. Put the zest into a jug, sprinkle with 2 tablespoons sugar, then squeeze the citrus juices and add to the jug. Fill with boiling water and let stand until cool. Taste and stir in extra sugar if necessary. Strain into a jug of ice and serve in long glasses filled with ice.

**VARIATIONS** *TANGERINEADE or LIMEADE*
Other citrus fruits can be made into lemonade-style drinks. Grate the zest of 6 tangerines or mandarins or 10 limes, leaving the white pith behind. Put the zest into a jug with a little sugar, then add the juice of all the fruit. Pour over 1 litre boiling water, let stand until cool, strain and serve over ice. You can also use less water and add soda water or mineral water when serving.

All fruits contain vitamin C, but oranges remain the benchmark against which all others are measured. Use them to extend fruits that don't have much juice themselves, such as blueberries, strawberries or apricots.

# lemon barley water

This soothing, cooling, old-fashioned drink is incredibly easy to make since the invention of the cafetière – the coffee maker with the plunger. In Victorian times, platoons of kitchen maids would boil up the lemon and barley, strain it through muslin into enormous pitchers, leave it to cool, then try to chill it with whatever technology was available in the Big House at the time. Lucky us – we have the cafetières and ice. So much easier! The Apple Water variation is wonderful.

*2 tablespoons pearl barley*
*grated zest and juice of 1 large, unwaxed lemon*
*2 teaspoons sugar*
*a curl of lemon peel*
*ice, to serve*

**SERVES 2–4**

Put the barley into a saucepan, add 1.5 litres boiling water and simmer for 30 minutes. Strain into a cafetière, then stir in the sugar, lemon zest and juice. Cool, plunge, chill, then serve over ice, decorated with a curl of lemon peel.

**VARIATION   *APPLE WATER***

Put the juice and zest of ½ lemon, 3 cored, sliced apples and 1 tablespoon sugar into a food processor and work to a purée. Transfer to a cafetière and pour over 750 ml boiling water. Cool, plunge and chill before serving.

# real lemonade

We've all had commercial lemonade, which is little more than fizzy sugar water. Real lemonade, on the other hand, is cool and refreshing and actually tastes of lemons. This recipe is a good old-fashioned lemonade, adapted from hand-written recipe books lent by aunts and grandmothers. It always reminds me of tennis parties, wicker chairs on the lawn, drinks in the cool shade of the verandah – and lemonade served by my mother, the last woman in the world to use a parasol!

*3–4 tablespoons sugar*
*1½ tablespoons lemon juice*
*a pinch of salt*
*mint leaves*
*a few slices of lemon*
*ice, to serve*

**SERVES 2–4**

Put the sugar and 125 ml water into a saucepan and boil for 2 minutes. Chill, then stir in the lemon juice and salt. Transfer to a large glass jug and add about 1 litre water. Add the mint leaves and lemon slices. Fill with ice, stir and serve.

Lemon juice is good for the digestion. Its sharp taste can also be used instead of salt to enhance other flavours.

# iced **lime tea**

*1 litre freshly made tea, lightly brewed*

*sugar, to taste*

*1–2 unwaxed limes, finely sliced*

*ice cubes*

*sparkling mineral water, lemonade or ginger ale*

**SERVES 4**

Strain the tea into a jug, stir in the sugar, cool and chill. Put sliced limes into a serving jug, then half-fill it with ice cubes. Half-fill the jug with the cold tea, then top up with mineral water, lemonade or ginger ale, stir and serve.

# hot **lemon tea**

*1 unwaxed lemon*

*1 tablespoon honey*

*1 pot of tea*

**SERVES 1**

Cut 2 slices off the lemon and squeeze the juice from the rest. Put the honey and sliced lemon into a large mug, add the lemon juice, then top with tea. Stir and drink.

# fresh lime soda

I have been to India many times, and it never seems to get any cooler!

My favourite thirst-quencher – served everywhere from five-star hotels to village truck-stops – is this fresh lime soda, served either with salt or sugar (or, in my case, plain).

Indian limes are inclined to be yellow, rather than green, and half the size of ordinary limes. They seem to be extra-juicy and not as tart as the green ones.

You wouldn't think that salty drinks could be at all pleasant, but Indians serve fresh lime sodas and yoghurt lassi drinks with a pinch of salt, and they are incredibly cooling. Try it and see!

*freshly squeezed juice of 1–2 limes*
*1 small bottle soda water*
*   or sparkling mineral water*
*sugar or sea salt, to taste*
*crushed ice or ice cubes (optional)*
**SERVES 1**

Put the lime juice into a tall glass. Serve with a bottle of soda water or fizzy mineral water, and small dishes of salt or sugar, according to taste. Crushed ice or ice cubes may also be added.

# citron pressé

Surprisingly, the French version, the Citron Pressé, is very similar to Fresh Lime Soda. Lemon juice is squeezed into a glass, and served with a separate jug of iced water and a bowl of sugar. I think this is just the perfect cooler in the middle of a hard day's shopping in Paris!

*1 lemon, squeezed*

**to serve**
*a small jug of iced water*
*sugar*
**SERVES 1**

Put the lemon juice into a tall glass and put onto a small plate with a small napkin under the glass. Serve with a jug of iced water, a small dish of sugar and a long spoon.

Lemons and limes are high in vitamin C and become sweeter and juicier as they ripen. They have an antibacterial and decongestant action, so are excellent for coughs and colds.

# banana and honey breakfast smoothie

A filling breakfast – full of flavour, packed with calcium and fibre and very good for you! If you like your drinks less sweet, reduce the quantity of honey. You can also substitute other fruit in season, such as berries. Use chilled fruit to make smoothies, but never keep bananas in the refrigerator – or anywhere near citrus fruit – they don't like it. They quickly turn black in the refrigerator, and become over-ripe in a flash if introduced to a citrus fruit.

*250 ml low-fat milk*
*250 ml low-fat yoghurt*
*2 tablespoons crushed ice*
*1 tablespoon honey*
*1 banana*
*1 tablespoon wheatgerm*
**SERVES 2–4**

Put all the ingredients into a blender and blend until smooth. Add extra fruit if preferred.

# banana and papaya
## smoothie

Bananas and papayas won't juice effectively – their pulp is too dense – but they are definitely candidates for the blender treatment. If your blender doesn't crush ice, add it at the end, but, to help the machine run, you will need a little water, yoghurt or juice.

*1 small papaya, peeled, deseeded and*
*   cut into chunks*
*1 banana, peeled and cut into chunks*
*about 6 ice cubes*
*1 tablespoon wheatgerm (optional)*
*125 ml yoghurt or water (optional)*
**SERVES 2–4**

Put the papaya and banana into a blender with the ice and 125 ml water or yoghurt, if using. Blend until smooth, then add the wheatgerm, if using, and extra water or yoghurt to form a pourable consistency, then serve.

**VARIATION** Blueberries and banana make a famous combination. Blend them with ice, yoghurt and a dash of honey.

Bananas are high in complex carbohydrates —
that's why you see tennis players eating them
at Wimbledon. Very nourishing and good for
your cholesterol levels.

# banana
## and coconut
### shake

Coconut milk and bananas are a traditional Thai combination – I've added dark rum as an optional extra. The result is a Thailand-meets-the-Caribbean mixture!

*about 250 ml canned coconut milk*
*250 ml low-fat milk*
*2 ripe bananas, cut into chunks*
*1 tablespoon dark rum, or to taste (optional)*
*sugar, to taste*
*crushed ice, to serve*

**SERVES 1–2**

Put the coconut milk into a blender, then add the milk, bananas and rum, if using. Blend until smooth, then add sugar to taste (and extra rum if you like). Blend again, then pour over crushed ice and serve.

# bananas
## and limes with
### ginger ale

Bananas and limes are typical South-east Asian ingredients, as is ginger, though not usually in this form. Lychees, if you can find them, make a delicious substitute for the bananas – they are sold either fresh or canned in Asian markets.

*2–3 large bananas, cut into chunks*
*grated zest and juice of 2 limes*
*ginger ale, to taste*
*sugar, to taste*
*crushed ice, to serve*

**SERVES 2**

Put the bananas into a blender, then add the lime zest and juice and a little ginger ale. Blend well, then taste and add sugar to taste. Half-fill the glasses with crushed ice, pour over the mixture and top up with more ginger ale.

Bananas are energy foods – rich in potassium, vitamins A, C and K. They can be meal in themselves – wonderful for breakfast and good for growing children.

# pineapple and lime crush

To keep cut pineapple in the refrigerator, wrap it in clingfilm to prevent it tainting other foods. Fruit varies in sweetness, so taste the crush before serving and add sugar to taste. This drink is also great made with ice cream instead of the yoghurt or coconut milk, though you will have to add a little chilled milk or the drink will be too thick.

*300 ml yoghurt or coconut milk*

*250 g chopped fresh ripe pineapple\**

*juice and grated rind of 2 limes*

*250 ml crushed ice*

*sugar, to taste*

*finely sliced fresh coconut (optional)*

*1 scoop vanilla ice cream (optional)*

**SERVES 1–2**

Put the first 4 ingredients into a blender and purée until smooth. Add sugar to taste and serve topped with fresh coconut or ice cream, if using.

**\*Note**  If you haven't done it before, peeling a pineapple can be tricky. Put the pineapple on its side with the prickly top hanging over the edge of the table. Grasp it firmly and jerk it down – the top will come off. Discard it. Cut off both ends to make them flat, then put the pineapple on the flat bottom. Slice the skin off vertically, cut out the prickly 'eyes' with the tip of a sharp knife, then cut into wedges and cut out and discard the cores.

# banana, honey and soy milk smoothie

A good breakfast smoothie – and full of protein from the soy milk. It is quite sweet, so taste the mixture before adding any extra honey. Other fruits, such as strawberries or papaya, can be used instead of the banana.

*1 banana, cut into chunks*

*1 teaspoon honey*

*250 ml soy milk*

*250 ml crushed ice (optional)*

*sprigs of mint, to serve (optional)*

**SERVES 1**

Put the banana, honey and soy milk into a blender with the crushed ice, if using, and blend until smooth. Serve, topped with sprigs of mint.

# pineapple crush

*1 large pineapple*

*1 lemon*

*ice cubes*

*4 passionfruit (optional)*

*sugar or honey, to taste*

**SERVES 4**

Peel the pineapple as on the previous page. Cut it into wedges, then chunks, then press through a juicer. Add the juice of 1 lemon and pour the mixture into a jug of ice. Stir in the flesh and seeds of 3 passionfruit, if using, and top with the remaining flesh and seeds. Depending on the sweetness and ripeness of the pineapple, you may like to add a little sugar or honey.

Fresh pineapple contains the enzyme bromelian, which helps with digestion. It is soothing for sore throats, coughs and upset stomachs.

Eating ripe fresh mangoes is good for your skin and for high blood pressure. Mangoes are better blended rather than juiced and are good mixed with other ingredients, such as coconut milk or yoghurt.

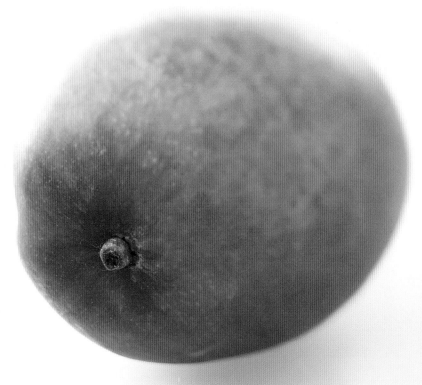

## mango
### ginger lassi

This mango lassi is made with the Indian Alphonso – the world's greatest mango. If you can't find him fresh, purée any variety of sweet mango in a blender. The good-quality canned Alphonso mango purée sold by Asian grocers can also be used instead (and tastes spectacular).

*250 ml mango purée\**
*250 ml low-fat plain yoghurt*
*1 tablespoon ginger purée (pages 49, 79)*
*crushed ice*
*1 litre ginger beer*
**SERVES 6–8 OR MORE**

Put the first 4 ingredients into a jug and mix well (I use a pair of chopsticks). Top up with ginger beer and serve.

**\*Note**  You can also use frozen mango – just put 250 g into a blender with a few tablespoons of water and blend until smooth.

# mango and
## coconut milk

A nut-milk recipe that's particularly good for people who are lactose-intolerant – and for anyone lucky enough to have too many mangoes.

*2 fresh ripe mangoes, peeled and pitted,*
   *or 250 ml mango purée (page 44)*
*juice of ½ lime or lemon*
*250 ml desiccated coconut (measured by*
   *volume), or canned coconut milk*

**SERVES 2**

Blend the mangoes with the lime or lemon juice, then transfer to a jug and chill.

If using desiccated coconut, put it into a blender with 250 ml iced water. Blend until frothy, let stand for 5 minutes, then blend again. Strain into the jug and return the coconut to the blender. Repeat with another 250 ml iced water. Strain, then stir into the jug of mango and lime or lemon. Serve immediately. Alternatively, omit the coconut milk and just blend the mango and lime or lemon juice with enough ice cubes and water to make a pourable consistency.

When properly ripe, mango skin can be removed a little like a banana skin. If you have to peel it with a knife, it's not ripe enough.

# watermelon
## and ginger sharbat

Indian and Moroccan sharbats are distantly related to the sherbets which are familiar to Westerners. They were introduced to India by the Moghul emperors who invaded over its North-west Frontier in the 16th century.

If you have a juicer, use it to make watermelon juice – though, I must admit, I sometimes prefer the thicker consistency produced by a food processor. You can buy ginger purée in supermarkets, but, if you can't find it, just peel and slice fresh ginger and purée in a food processor with a little water or lemon juice, then freeze in ice cube trays for future use.

*1 small, ripe watermelon, chilled*
*2 tablespoons ginger purée, or to taste*
*sugar, to taste*
*crushed ice, to serve*
**SERVES 2–4**

Cut the watermelon in half, then remove and discard the rind and seeds. Put the watermelon flesh and ginger into a food processor and blend until smooth. Add water if the mixture is too thick. Taste and add sugar if needed, then serve over crushed ice.

# watermelon
## and lime slush

Turn your sharbat into a slush, a frappé or a granita, and point up the flavour with a little lime juice.

*1 small, ripe watermelon, chilled*
*5 cm fresh ginger, peeled and grated*
*crushed ice*
*2 limes, cut into wedges*
**SERVES 4**

Prepare the watermelon and ginger as in the previous recipe and put the flesh through a juicer. Serve in glasses half-filled with crushed ice and top with wedges of lime for squeezing.

To make a frappé or granita, add sugar to taste (the mixture should be very sweet), then freeze in small, shallow containers. Just before serving, crush into icy shards and serve as a granita at the end of a meal. Alternatively, crush into an icy slush and serve as a frappé drink.

Many fruit juices can be frozen, then crushed with a fork to form a granita to serve in a bowl, or crushed further to form a frappé, served as a drink.

# melon froth

The four melon varieties used in this
drink are my favourites and all very
aromatic. My juicer produces a froth,
but if yours is less muscular, you
could layer the juices to form orange
and green stripes. Wonderful for
a summer brunch party.

*1–2 melons – orange cantaloupe or charentais,*
    *or green galia or honeydew, halved, deseeded*
    *and peeled*
*ginger syrup, to taste (optional)*
**SERVES 1–2**

Put the melons through a juicer. Layer the colours
in glasses if preferred, or serve separately. If using
ginger syrup, serve it separately.

Melons have a delicate, elusive flavour and a delightful texture. Melon and ginger is one of the great food marriages, so a dash of ground ginger or fresh ginger juice is utterly wonderful.

# apple
## lemonade

This recipe is best made with cooking apples – they turn to delicious apple-flavoured foam when boiled.

For a much quicker result, use fresh apple juice, omit the sugar, add the fresh lemon juice and fill with mineral water.

*2–3 cooking apples, unpeeled,*
*chopped into small pieces*
*sugar, to taste*
*juice of 1 lemon*

**to serve**
*sparkling mineral water*
*ice*
**SERVES 4**

Put the apples into a saucepan, cover with cold water, bring to the boil and simmer until soft. Strain, pressing the pulp through the strainer with a spoon. Add sugar to taste, stir until dissolved, then let cool.

To serve, pack a jug with ice, half-fill the glass with the apple juice, add the lemon juice and top with sparkling mineral water.

Cooked apple drinks are usually pale, but fresh juices made from red apples will be pink if you juice them with the skins on.

# apple juice
## with fennel

Fennel can be very difficult to juice –
you need a strong machine. Alternatively,
chop it and purée in a blender with apple
juice, then strain. Use a crisp, sweet,
red apple such as Red Delicious to give
a wonderful pinkish tinge. Always
remember to remove the stem and stalk
ends of apples and pears, where any
pesticides and residues collect.

*1 fennel bulb, including sprigs of the*
*    feathery leaves*
*2 apples, cored but not peeled*
*juice of ½ lemon (optional)*
**SERVES 1–2**

Trim the green leaves from the fennel bulb, trim off
the root end, then slice the bulb into long wedges
and cut out and remove the cores from each
wedge. Cut the apple into wedges. Put the apples
and fennel through a juicer.

Stir in the lemon juice to stop discoloration, then
serve immediately, topped with a few fennel sprigs
for extra scent.

# minty
## ginger
### granny smith

Any apples will do, but unpeeled Granny Smiths produce the most beautiful green. The ginger is optional, but utterly delicious, and the mint leaves give an even brighter green. Just a hint – we professional dieters know to use apple juice instead of sugar to add sweetness. Lime juice will stop the apple juice turning brown so quickly, but drink this concoction immediately – don't let it hang around, or you lose all the benefits of freshly crushed juice.

*4 Granny Smith apples, cored but not peeled,*
*    then cut into chunks*
*a chunk of fresh ginger, peeled and sliced*
*4–8 sprigs of mint*
*1 tablespoon fresh lime juice (optional)*
**SERVES 1**

Push half the apples through a juicer, then the ginger, mint and lime juice, if using. Finally, push through the remaining apples and serve.

**VARIATION** *FROZEN APPLE MARGARITA*
Put 250 ml crushed ice into a blender, add the juice and blend to a froth. The Margarita is ready when the sound of the motor changes – that means the mixture has risen away from the blades.

Apples are particularly good for the heart and blood and can help to lower cholesterol levels.

# vegetable magic

Most vegetables are better for you uncooked, because cooking destroys many vitamins, such as vitamin C. Salads and crudités are good ways to serve them, but juicing is probably the quickest and easiest way of all. There are many inexpensive juicers on the market now: I keep mine out on the worktop and use it every day to make fruit and vegetable juices. Perfect for breakfast!

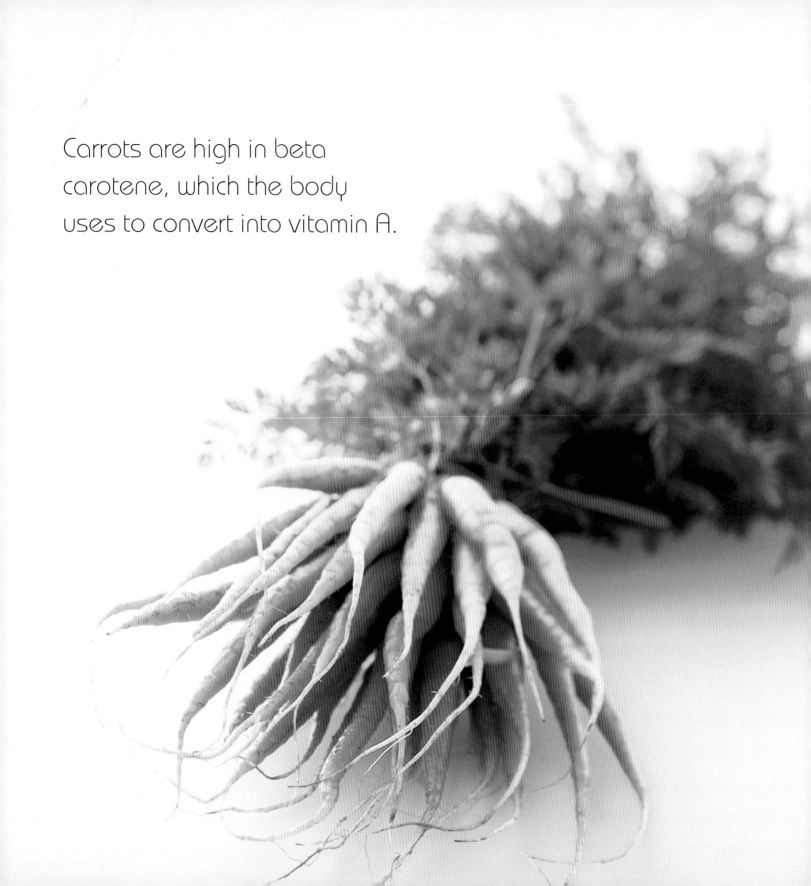

Carrots are high in beta carotene, which the body uses to convert into vitamin A.

# carrot and
## ginger crush

Carrot juice, so naturally sweet, is my
absolutely favourite juice. Though
carrots are better for you when cooked,
I much prefer them raw. Just make sure
you peel them first, unless they have
been organically grown.

*5 medium carrots, peeled*
*a chunk of fresh ginger, peeled and sliced*
  *(optional)*
**SERVES 1–2**

Cut the carrots into pieces small enough to fit
through the feeder tube. When half the carrots
have been processed, add the ginger, if using,
then the rest of the carrots.

**Note**  Don't drink carrot juice more than
2–3 times a week, or your skin may develop an
orange, carroty tinge!

## tomato, celery and **carrot** crush

Juicers are wonderful machines. Fresh foaming carrot juice is my favourite, but try this spicy combination too. You could substitute 2 deseeded chillies instead of the Tabasco sauce, for a fresh, bright chilli taste. Chill all the vegetables first, for a summer cooler.

*1 kg carrots*

*3 celery stalks*

*500 g tomatoes*

*salt and freshly ground black pepper*

*Tabasco sauce, to taste*

*crushed ice, to serve*

**SERVES 4–6**

Push the carrots, celery and tomatoes through a juicer. Alternatively, purée in a food processor with 250 ml iced water, then press through a strainer. Add salt, pepper and Tabasco, to taste. Serve poured over crushed ice.

The tomato is one of the healthiest of all vegetables – what better excuse to have a Bloody Mary? Mixed with carrots and celery, it's a real vitamin powerhouse.

## celery and grapes

Celery juice is marvellous when mixed with other vegetable juices – and also with juicy fruits such as grapes. You can buy grape juice, but fresh juice is a revelation. White grapes will produce a fresh green juice – red or black ones a delicious pink-tinged nectar.

*6 celery stalks, trimmed*

*about 20 seedless white grapes*

*1 bunch watercress (optional)*

*ice cubes*

**SERVES 1–2**

Push the celery stalks into the juicer, leaf end first. Alternate with the grapes, which are very soft and difficult to push through on their own. Press through the watercress, if using, and serve plain, in glasses filled with ice, or put into a blender with ice cubes to produce a delicious celery-grape froth.

Celery has almost no calories – it's like eating water, so is marvellous for dieters. Celery is also a natural tranquilizer, so sip and snooze.

Peppers and their hot-headed chilli cousins have three times as much vitamin C as an orange. Juicing removes the indigestible skins and extracts all the sweet flavour.

## mexican
# golden
### salsa crush

Peppers, tomatoes and chillies originally came from Mexico. I am not very fond of fiery-hot chillies, so one medium-hot one is plenty for me. Add more if you like, or use a hotter one. the pinch of salt is optional, but salt will point up the flavour beautifully. If you're a proponent of the salt-free diet, try a dash of freshly squeezed lemon juice instead.

*2 red, orange or yellow peppers,*
*    halved and deseeded*
*1 medium-hot red chilli, deseeded*
*2 tomatoes, quartered*
*a pinch of salt or a squeeze of lemon juice*
*    (optional)*
*ice, to serve (optional)*
**SERVES 1**

Push 1 pepper through the juicer, then the chilli, tomatoes and salt or lemon juice, if using. Push through the remaining pepper and serve immediately, over ice, if using.

# beetroot
## and orange juice

Raw beetroot is good for you, but only in small quantities – and it has a decidedly earthy taste. Trimming and peeling before juicing will help, but I like to 'stretch' it with freshly squeezed juice such as orange or even apple. Depending on the sweetness of the oranges, you may need a little honey as well.

*1 medium beetroot, trimmed and peeled*
*2–3 oranges*
*honey, to taste*
**SERVES 1**

Cut the beetroot into pieces and press through a juicer. Squeeze the oranges. Mix and taste, adding honey if necessary.

**Note:** Beetroot leaves are also delicious – juice them separately or with spinach leaves. Alternatively, sauté in a little olive oil and serve as an accompaniment to main courses.

Beetroot, famous as a blood tonic, is a powerhouse of vitamins and minerals. It is good for blood pressure, protects against anaemia and promotes general good health.

# lettuce and
## parsley crush

Lettuce and parsley produce small quantities of juice and taste decidedly green! So add the juice of an apple or other fruit as an extender and sweetener. As many good cooks know, much of the flavour in parsley is in the stalks, so juice them too. Before juicing, all leafy vegetables should be washed well, wrapped in a cloth and chilled until crisp.

*1 cos or iceberg lettuce, stalk trimmed*

*1 large bunch of parsley, including stalks,*
    *ends trimmed*

*1 green apple, cored and quartered,*
    *but not peeled*

**SERVES 1**

Form the lettuce and parsley leaves into balls and push through the feed tube of the juicer. Push the apple through (this will extract more juice from the lettuce and parsley). Stir if necessary, then serve immediately – don't wait.

Parsley is famous as a breath freshener and an effective digestive. Lettuce is high in antioxidants – and iceberg is a particularly juicy variety. Cucumber is low in calories but rich in vitamins B1, B2 and C and the minerals calcium and iron.

# cucumber juice
## with spinach

Spinach is high in iron, but not in a form easily used by the body. In fact, too much isn't good for you. It got its 'ironic' reputation because, when the original testing was done in the 1800s, someone got the decimal point in the wrong place and the mistake wasn't discovered until it was retested in 1947. Drinking spinach juice is no-one's idea of a good time, but if you mix it with something more delicious you'll absorb all its goodness almost painlessly. Apple or cucumber are both good choices. If using cucumbers, try to use organically grown produce. Others are often waxed and must be peeled first (so you lose some of the colour and nutrients).

*1 organic cucumber, about 30 cm long,*
*    quartered lengthways*
*1 large handful of well-washed spinach*
*salt or lemon juice, to taste (optional)*
**SERVES 1–2**

Juice half the cucumber, then all the spinach, then the remaining cucumber. Add salt or lemon juice to taste, if using.

**VARIATION** Cucumber has a cooling, astringent effect – to sweeten it, use half-and-half with apple juice from crisp Granny Smiths.

# herbs, spices and nuts

Herbs and spices can add extra pizzazz to smoothies and fruit juices – and they're utterly gorgeous used to add flavour to tea, or to make an infusion. Many have healthful properties as well as tasting great. Nuts, ground with milk or water to make nut milk, were used as invalid food in olden times – these days, most cooks use them just for their flavour and their creamy, delicious smoothness.

# rosemary tisane

*Tisane* is a French word which means an infusion of herbs, flowers or leaves, usually dried – a kind of tea, in other words. I prefer tisanes made with fresh ingredients where possible. In early times, they were seen as cures for many ailments. Nowadays, people drink them because they taste good. A tisanière is a tall, lidded cup, with a strainer inside to hold the herb. If you don't have one (they can sometimes be found in antique shops), use a cafetière (coffee press) instead.

*4–6 sprigs of rosemary*
*1–2 teaspoons honey*
**SERVES 1–2**

Put the rosemary and honey into a cafetière or teapot, cover with boiling water, let infuse for about 5 minutes, then plunge or strain.

**VARIATIONS** Tisanes can also be made with camomile flowers, lemon balm, marjoram, sage, thyme and orange blossoms.

Rosemary tea will wake you up, so drink it only in the morning (it's also good for a hangover). Lavender is mildly sedative, so it's good to drink before bed or when you need to relax.

## lavender tea

The very essence of a hot summer afternoon in Italy or the South of France, lavender tea is wonderfully calming for frazzled nerves: drink it after a hard day at the office, or sip a cup before bed.

*1–2 large sprigs of lavender leaves*
*a few lavender flowers, if available*
*1 teaspoon honey, or to taste*
**SERVES 1**

Put the lavender into a teapot or one-cup cafetière and and cover with boiling water. Let steep for about 5 minutes, covered. Put 1 teaspoon honey, if using, into your cup, then press the plunger and pour the tea.

Alternatively, pour the honey over the lavender in the cafetière before adding the boiling water.

# moroccan iced
## mint tea

Moroccan mint tea is served hot in tiny engraved and gilded glasses – it's the perfect finish to a spicy Moroccan meal and helps oil the wheels of conversation in countless tea shops across the land. I like it hot in the traditional way, but it's also marvellous chilled and iced as a cool summer drink.

I prefer to make it in a cafetière, then you don't have to bother with straining or fishing out the leaves. If you don't have a cafetière, you can also make it in a big teapot or jug, then strain into a second jug before chilling and serving.

*1 large bunch of fresh mint*
*2 tablespoons leaf tea, such as*
  *Earl Grey or green tea*

**to serve**
*mint sprigs*
*sugar*
**SERVES 4–6**

Fill a cafetière with mint, add the tea and pour over boiling water. Let brew for 1–2 minutes (no longer or the tannin will be released from the tea). Push the plunger. To serve hot, pour into small tea glasses with a dish of sugar served separately.

To serve cold, pour the tea into a jug. Chill until very cold, then serve in tea glasses with mint and the dish of sugar.

Endless glasses of this aromatic brew drive animated conversations in the tea houses of Morocco. Like tea, mint is a stimulant, so don't drink it late at night. However, like ginger, it will help digestion and relieve an upset stomach.

# mint tisane

*1 large bunch of mint*
*sugar or honey, to taste (optional)*
**SERVES 1–4**

Wash the mint well, then break it into large
handfuls and put into a cafetière. Pour over boiling
water, let steep for 3–5 minutes, then press the
plunger. Pour into tea glasses, add sugar or honey,
if using, and a few fresh mint leaves, then serve.

## mint and
# ginger
## yoghurt soda

Mint and ginger make a gorgeous combination. Ginger purée is sold in some supermarkets – or make it yourself with fresh root ginger in a blender. Plain yoghurt has a wonderful lemony taste. I prefer this drink without sugar – so taste it first and decide for yourself.

*300 ml plain or low-fat yoghurt*

*leaves from 4 sprigs of mint*

*2.5 cm piece of fresh ginger, grated, or*

  *1 tablespoon ginger purée*

*500 ml sparkling mineral water, or to taste*

*sugar, to taste*

*crushed ice, to serve*

**SERVES 2–4**

Put the yoghurt, mint and ginger into a blender, add about 100 ml sparkling water and blend to a froth. Add sugar if preferred. Spoon crushed ice into each glass, pour over the mixture, then top up with more sparkling water.

## pineapple
## with jamaican
# ginger beer

Ginger beer is a favourite drink in Jamaica. Put it together with fresh pineapple and you have an utterly delicious thirst-quencher – the taste of the Caribbean through a straw! Try it mixed with other fresh fruit too, such as very ripe peaches, papayas or apricots.

*3 slices ripe fresh pineapple, chilled*

*about 250 ml ginger beer, chilled*

*about 250 ml crushed ice*

**SERVES 1–2**

Put the pineapple into a blender, add about 2–3 tablespoons of the ginger beer, then the crushed ice. Blend well, then pour into tall glasses or mugs and top up with the remaining ginger beer.

# ginger tea

*a chunk of fresh ginger*
*1 teaspoon leaf tea (optional)*
*sweetener of your choice*
**SERVES 1**

Peel and grate the ginger. (The cheese-grater
shown here is quick, clean and easy.) Put into a
tea strainer or tea ball set in the cup, then add the
tea, if using. Add boiling water and let steep for
1–5 minutes, according to how strong you like the
flavour. Add sweetener if you like, then sip slowly.
The same ginger can be used for extra cups.

**VARIATION** If you're short of time, you don't even
need to grate the ginger – just slice it into a cup,
then add boiling water.

## jamaican
# iced ginger
### sorrel tea

Jamaican sorrel is the flower of a native hibiscus, sold fresh or dried in Caribbean stores or in health food shops, where it is sometimes labelled as 'red hibiscus tea'. In Australia and New Zealand, it's known as 'rosella' and is used to make jam. It's an unusual, sophisticated taste – not unlike cranberry juice – and, if you like vaguely bitter flavours, you'll love it!

Of course most things Caribbean will go with a swing if you add a good measure of rum. My favourite is a gorgeous golden rum called Mount Gay, but there are others. I prefer golden or dark because they seem to have more flavour than white rum.

*3 cm fresh ginger, peeled and sliced or grated*
*4 tablespoons dried sorrel flowers or hibiscus tea*
*4 tablespoons sugar*

**to serve**
*ice*
*a twist of lime*

**SERVES 4–8**

Put the ginger, sorrel and sugar into a cafetière. Pour over boiling water. When the liquid is a light purple (this happens fast!) push the plunger, then serve immediately, or cool and chill. Serve over ice with a twist of lime. To serve as a longer drink, top up with ginger ale, soda or mineral water. The cocktail below usually has lots of sugar, but I prefer it less sweet.

**VARIATION  *SORREL RUM COCKTAIL***
Put 4 tablespoons dried sorrel, a twist of orange peel, 1 cinnamon stick, 6 cloves and 200–400 g sugar into a cafetière. Pour over 1.5 litres boiling water, stir well, then push the plunger. Add 2 extra cloves and a cinnamon stick to the top, cool and chill. To serve, pour over ice, then add a jigger of rum and a cinnamon stick for swizzling.

Dried red sorrel flowers are sold in Caribbean markets – use by themselves to make tea, or add other Caribbean flavours like ginger and lime.

## fresh homemade
# ginger beer

Our family made ginger beer when I was a kid – the cupboards in the kitchen and the barn always seemed to be full of bottles, which sometimes exploded spectacularly over a period of weeks, as the ginger beer fermented.

This ginger beer is quicker than the traditional kind and I also think the taste is fresher and brighter. Don't peel the ginger if you're blending it in a food processor – just chop it up coarsely, then pulse until well chopped. The skin will give the beer extra flavour.

*125 g grated fresh ginger*
*zest and juice of 2 limes*
*2 cloves*
*200 g sugar (brown gives better colour)*
*soda water or sparkling mineral water, to serve*
**SERVES 4**

Put all the ingredients into a large cafetière or heatproof jug, pour over 1 litre boiling water and stir until the sugar dissolves.

Cool, plunge or strain, then chill well. To serve, half-fill glasses with the mixture and top with soda water or sparkling mineral water.

Ginger isn't just one of the world's great flavours – delicious in sweet or savoury dishes – it is also a healthy wonderfood. It is most famous for its ability to calm an upset stomach and soothe indigestion, coughs and colds. However, it's also a popular folk remedy to help ease the pain of arthritis.

# cardamom

## green tea

In India, tea is usually made with milk, but in the far north, which had trading links with China, they sometimes use green tea. I discovered this recipe there: a pot of green tea containing an aromatic treasure – a spoonful of green cardamom pods. Often you find a few pods stuffed down the spout of the teapot, so the boiling tea picks up gorgeous flavours as it passes over the spice. If you need an excuse to drink it, remember that, like ginger, cardamom is also a powerful soothing agent for upset stomachs.

*1 teaspoon green tea, plus 1 for the pot*
*6 green cardamom pods*
*sugar, to taste*
**SERVES 2**

Rinse the teapot with boiling water, add the tea and cardamom, then fill with boiling water. Let steep for 1–2 minutes only (no longer, or the bitter tannins will be released). Pour the tea and add sugar only if you usually like sweet tea.

Cardamom is the basis of 'chai masala' – an aromatic blend of spices used to flavour tea all over India. Make up your own mixture, adding ginger, cinnamon, cloves and other favourites.

# star anise tea

If you like aniseed flavours, like liquorice or pastis, you'll love this drink. Tea is always best made with leaves, but this recipe can also be made with your favourite brand of tea bag. I like it not too strong and served without milk.

*1 tea bag, such as English Breakfast*
*1 whole star anise*
*sweetener, to taste*
*milk (optional)*
**SERVES 1**

Put the tea bag and star anise into a cup, add sweetener if you usually use it, then pour over boiling water. Let steep for your usual amount of time, then remove the tea bag and serve, with milk, if using.

## coconut milkshake
## with **cloves**

I've used ordinary canned coconut milk in this recipe. However, if you'd like to make your own coconut milk, put about 8 oz. desiccated coconut into a bowl and cover with milk or water. Let stand for 20 minutes, then press through a strainer. If you don't want to use coconut milk at all, substitute ordinary milk plus coconut syrup, or any kind of fruit syrup.

*100 ml milk*

*250 ml canned coconut milk*

*3 scoops ice cream*

*1 teaspoon ground cloves*

*sugar, to taste*

**to serve (optional)**

*crushed ice*

*finely sliced fresh coconut*

**SERVES 1–2**

Put the milk, coconut milk, ice cream and cloves into a blender and blend until frothy. Taste and add sugar if required.

Blend again until the sugar has dissolved. Serve over crushed ice, topped with coconut.

Cloves were originally a medicinal spice, supposed to guard against the plague and, for good measure, also regarded as an aphrodisiac. Christmas oranges studded with cloves were originally a talisman against illness.

# almond sharbat

The sharbat is the ancestor of sherbet – cool, thirst-quenching and perfect for people who don't drink alcohol. They can be made with either nuts or fruits, as in Watermelon Sharbat (page 49).

*125 g blanched almonds*
*a few drops of almond essence (optional)*
*1 teaspoon rosewater (optional)*
*crushed seeds from 8 green cardamom pods*
*sugar, to taste*

**SERVES 1–2**

Put the almonds into a blender, grind to a meal, then add enough water to make a smooth paste. Add the almond essence and rosewater, if using, then the cardamom seeds, 500 ml cold water and sugar to taste. Blend well, taste and add sugar if necessary, then serve poured over crushed ice. Blend, then taste and add more sugar if liked. Pour over crushed ice and serve.

# almond milk

You can use unblanched almonds (with their skins still on), but the result is browner and grittier. To blanch your own almonds, put into a bowl, cover with boiling water, leave for 5 minutes, then pop them out of their skins.

*1 small packet almonds, preferably blanched, about 100 g*
*1 tablespoon honey*
*250 ml ice cubes or crushed ice, to serve*

**SERVES 1–2**

Put the almonds and honey into a blender, then add the ice cubes and 250 ml iced water. Blend to a paste. Gradually add extra iced water until the mixture is smooth. Strain and serve over ice.

Nut milks are wonderful for people who 'don't do dairy'. You can make them with any nuts, but almonds are easy to find. Almond milk was an old-fashioned invalid food: if you're healthy, it will obviously make you even stronger!

# clever cocktails

Fruit and fruit juices, spices – and even vegetables, in the
case of a Bloody Mary – can all be turned into gorgeous
cocktails and long drinks with mixers. Use the ideas here as
a base and let your imagination run wild. Usually, all you
need is a blender, but sometimes just a cocktail shaker
will do. Choose your favourite fruit, then blend it with ice
and spirit or liqueur – or pour over chilled champagne or
wine and you have a perfect summer drink.

# frozen margarita

Margaritas are my favourite cocktail. They're great but lethal when made properly and, I've found, sometimes almost totally without alcohol when ordered in a bar (probably a good idea!). The usual way of serving margaritas is to dip the rim of the glasses in salt – this is optional, but I think that a twist of lime is absolutely crucial! Some people also like a dash of sugar – though, in my opinion, this depends on the flavour of the limes.

*75 ml freshly squeezed lime juice, plus extra*
  *for the glass*
*salt, for the glass*
*75 ml Triple Sec or Cointreau*
*125 ml tequila*
*6 ice cubes ·*
*1 lime, halved and finely sliced lengthways,*
  *to serve*
*salt for the glass*
**SERVES 4**

Dip the rim of each glass onto a saucer of lime juice, then into a second saucer of salt.

Put the lime juice, Triple Sec or Cointreau and tequila into a blender with crushed ice. Blend until frothy. The sound of the motor will suddenly change as the froth rises above the blades.

Pour into the chilled, salt-rimmed Margarita glasses and serve with a slice of lime.

# strawberry margarita

*1 punnet ripe strawberries (about 12)*
*250 ml tequila*
*1 tablespoon powdered sugar or caster sugar*
*juice of 1 lime*
*1 tablespoon strawberry syrup*
*6 ice cubes*
**SERVES 6**

Put all the ingredients into a blender with crushed ice. Blend and serve as in the previous recipe.

# cranberry margarita

*50 ml tequila*
*50 ml Cointreau or Triple Sec*
*juice of ½ lime*
*100 ml cranberry juice*
*6 ice cubes*
*sugar, to taste*
**SERVES 2**

Put all the ingredients except the sugar into a blender. Blend well, then add sugar to taste.

# watermelon gin

I grew up in the tropics, where there were lots of different watermelon varieties. The round ones with dark green skins and orange-red flesh were called sugar-melons, but the enormous torpedo-shaped watermelons, with striped skins and pinky-red flesh, were our favourites.

The seed-free section in the middle of a melon is the sweetest, so if you're cutting pieces for garnish, use this part.

*2 very ripe watermelons, well chilled*
*500–750 ml gin (or to taste)*
*crushed ice, to serve*
*sprigs of mint, to serve*
*watermelon triangles, to serve (optional)*
**SERVES 10–20**

Cut the watermelon in half and remove the rind and seeds. Working in batches, put the flesh into a blender or food processor and blend until smooth. If the mixture is too thick, add water.

Pour into a jug and stir in the gin. Fill glasses with ice, pour over the Watermelon Gin and serve topped with a sprig of mint and a melon triangle.

**VARIATION** *LIME AND WATERMELON VODKA*
Substitute vodka instead of the gin, and stir in the juice of 2 limes.

**Note** Some people blend the watermelon with the seeds still in it, then strain it before serving. I think this spoils the flavour and appearance, and most of the creamy solids are removed during straining. It's well worth taking the time to remove the seeds.

The summery flavour of ripe, red watermelon goes wonderfully well with the fresh, clean, lemony taste of gin.

# blueberry gin

A delicious drink based on sloe gin, which is made in autumn, then set aside until Christmas. I think it should be served in small glasses – it tastes wonderful, but is very heady, and can be something of a trap. You can also serve it in long glasses with ice and tonic water. Delicious and the most marvellous colour!

*1 punnet blueberries*

*6 tablespoons sugar*

*1 large bottle gin, 750 ml*

*crushed ice, to serve (optional)*

*Indian tonic water, to serve (optional)*

*sprigs of mint, to serve (optional)*

**SERVES 15–20**

Put the blueberries into a large glass bottle or empty bottle of spirits. Add the sugar and gin, then shake well and set aside for at least 2 weeks, or up to 2 months. Shake the bottle from time to time – you will see the marvellous rich colour developing as the days go by.

Put a shot of the gin into a blender with 3 tablespoons of crushed ice. Blend, then pour into long chilled glasses. Add a sprig of mint and tonic to taste.

Alternatively, serve alone in small aquavit-style or shot glasses. Do not drive!

One of the great English Christmastime drinks is sloe gin, made with the fruit of the blackthorn, gathered in the hedgerows in autumn, after the first frost. If you don't have a hedgerow handy, blueberries make a delicious substitute.

# bloody mary

Make Bloody Mary with fresh tomato juice and your friends will love you forever. Fresh tomato juice is thinner and sweeter than the commercial kinds – and more delicious. I make my tomato juice in a blender – tomatoes are hard to push through a juicer because they are so pulpy. If you do try it, push the celery stalks through alternately with the tomatoes: the fibrous celery will help push through the tomatoes.

*6 ripe tomatoes*

*3 celery stalks, coarsely chopped*

*1 garlic clove (optional)*

*1 red chilli, deseeded*

*a dash of Worcestershire sauce*

*2 measures vodka, or to taste*

*ice cubes, to serve*

**SERVES 2**

To skin the tomatoes, cut a small cross in the base, put into a large bowl and cover with boiling water. Leave for 1 minute, then drain and pull off the skins. Put the tomatoes, celery, garlic, if using, chilli, Worcestershire sauce and vodka into a blender and blend until smooth. Pour through a strainer into a jug of ice, then serve.

**VARIATION  *VIRGIN MARY***

Take any classic Bloody Mary recipe and omit the vodka. When you make it with the version above, with fresh tomato juice rather than juice from a bottle or can, it's especially delicious.

# bloody mary
## with chilli vodka

The spicy tastes of traditional Bloody Mary are usually provided by Tabasco sauce. However, you can provide the same spicy flavour by infusing fresh chillies in your bottle of vodka. Test the vodka after 1 day and remove the chilli if it's spicy enough. If not, leave for another couple of hours. Take care, and keep tasting, because you can easily make the vodka too hot!

*250 ml tomato juice*

*1 teaspoon Worcestershire sauce*

*1 tablespoon lemon juice*

*250 ml crushed ice*

**to serve**

*1 lemon wedge*

*1 celery stalk*

**chilli vodka**

*1 bottle vodka, 750 ml*

*2 serrano chillies, halved and deseeded*

**SERVES 1**

To make the chilli vodka, prick the chillies with a toothpick and gently slide them into the bottle of vodka. Set aside to infuse overnight. Taste, leave longer if liked, then remove and discard the chillies. Keep the vodka in the refrigerator.

To make the Bloody Mary, put the tomato juice into a blender with the Worcestershire sauce, lemon juice, 1 measure of chilli vodka and the crushed ice. Blend well, then pour into tall glasses and serve with a wedge of lemon and celery stalk.

# morocco mary

The absolutely best Bloody Mary you ever tasted! I promise you! I have served this recipe to Bloody Mary purists and it was a huge success. In trying to emulate my efforts, one particularly purist friend added the harissa paste to his regular spicy recipe and wondered why some of his guests looked decidedly overheated!

*1 teaspoon harissa paste*

*juice of 2 limes*

*75 ml vodka*

*250 ml tomato juice*

*salt and freshly ground black pepper*

*ice, to serve*

**SERVES 1–2**

Put the harissa, lime juice and vodka into a jug, mix well, then stir in the remaining ingredients.

Alternatively, put the harissa paste, tomato juice, lime juice, vodka, salt and pepper into a blender and blend well. Pour into a jug half-filled with ice and serve.

## swedish
# glögg

Glögg is the Scandinavian version of Christmas glühwein or mulled wine. (I much prefer it.)

*2 bottles dry red wine, 750 ml each*

*1 bottle aquavit or vodka, 750 ml*

*12 cardamom pods, crushed*

*8 whole cloves*

*1 orange*

*3 cm fresh ginger, sliced*

*1 cinnamon stick*

*250 g sugar*

*200 g blanched almonds*

*200 g raisins*

*cinnamon sticks, for stirring (optional)*

**SERVES ABOUT 20**

Using a vegetable peeler or cannelle knife, remove the peel from the orange in a single curl (do not include any of the bitter white pith).

Put everything except the almonds into a large stainless steel or enamel saucepan and set aside overnight (at least 12 hours).

Just before serving, heat to just below boiling point, then remove from the heat and stir in the almonds. Do not let boil or the alcohol will be burned off.

Serve in glass punch cups or tea glasses, with little spoons so people can scoop out the almonds and raisins. Small cinnamon sticks make delicious, scented stirrers.

## children's
# glögg

Why should children have all the fun? This is wonderful for non-imbibing adults as well.

*1 orange*

*1 litre apple cider (non-alcoholic)*

*500 ml apple juice*

*60 g caster sugar*

*1 cinnamon stick*

*5 whole cloves*

*75 g raisins\**

**SERVES 10**

Using a vegetable peeler or cannelle knife, remove the peel from the orange in a single curl (do not include any of the bitter white pith).

Put the orange peel and all the other ingredients into a large, stainless steel or enamel saucepan. Cover and set aside for 4 hours or overnight.

Just before the party, bring slowly to the boil over a gentle heat, then reduce to low and simmer for 30 minutes. Serve in punch cups or demitasse coffee cups, with some raisins in each serving.

**\*Note** The raisins can be strained out before serving if preferred. Traditionally this recipe also contains slivered almonds: I have omitted them because some children are allergic to nuts. If you like, share 75 g between the cups before serving.

# jamaican
## punch

This punch – great for a party – is very strong, so if you want to give people more than one glass, make it gentler by adding a bottle or two of ginger beer, ginger ale or mineral water. If you can't find ginger wine, use dry sherry, then add a chunk of fresh ginger, peeled and finely sliced.

*6 limes (3 juiced, 3 sliced)*
*½ bottle ginger wine, 375 ml*
*1 bottle white rum or vodka, 750 ml*
*sugar, to taste*
*3 lemons, sliced*
*1 starfruit, sliced (optional)*
*1 pineapple, cut lengthways into long wedges,*
   *then crossways into triangles*
*sprigs of mint, to serve*

**SERVES ABOUT 16–20**

Put the lime juice, ginger wine, rum or vodka and sugar into a jug and stir until the sugar dissolves.

Fill a punch bowl with ice, add the sliced fruit and pour over the ginger wine mixture. Stir well and serve with sprigs of mint.

## caribbean
# tea punch

Make this punch with a flavoured tea like Lapsang Souchong or Earl Grey. I make mine in a small cafetière so I can push the plunger as soon as the tea reaches the right colour – after 30 seconds to 1 minute, when the colour and flavour have developed, but before the bitter tannin is released.

The scent of lemon mixes beautifully with the richness of rum. For parties, make a big pot of tea, mix with half its volume of rum, then sweeten and serve with mixers.

*1 cup weak black tea*
*1 tablespoon caster sugar*
*crushed ice*
*125 ml dark rum or golden rum*
*peeled zest of ½ lemon*
*1 slice of lemon (optional)*
**SERVES 1–2**

Stir the sugar into the hot tea. Let cool, then stir well. Fill a glass with crushed ice, pour over the tea, stir in the rum and lemon zest, then serve with a slice of lemon, if using.

## mango
# rum punch

Many Caribbean punches are very strong, and this is one of them. I also like it turned into a party punch, served in a punch bowl and topped up with mixers.

*250 ml mango purée or 250 g frozen mango*
*1 teaspoon lemon juice*
*a pinch of ground cardamom\**
*500 ml golden rum*
*6 ice cubes*
*black seeds from 3 green cardamom pods*
**SERVES 10**

Put the mango or mango purée into a blender with the lemon juice, ground cardamom and rum. Add the ice cubes and blend until smooth. Strain into chilled glasses, filled with ice if preferred, and top with a few cardamom seeds, if using.

**\*Note**  For the best cardamom, crush 6 green pods with a mortar and pestle, extract the black seeds and discard the green pods. Grind the pods to a powder using a mortar and pestle.

## planter's
# punch

There must be hundreds of combinations for Planter's Punch, and their composition probably depended on where the planter lived – this one comes from sugar-growing areas such as Australia and the Caribbean.

*250 ml white rum*
*250 ml pineapple juice (freshly crushed,*
*  if possible)*
*250 ml mango purée or mango juice*
*grated zest and juice of 1 large lime*
*a dash of Angostura Bitters*
*1 cinnamon stick*
*ice, to serve*
**SERVES 3–6**

Put the rum into a large jug, then add the pineapple juice, mango purée or mango juice, the lime zest and juice and the Bitters. Stir and serve over ice, with a cinnamon swizzle stick.

The daiquiri was born in Cuba and traditionally uses light Cuban rum. It can also be made from a special rum called 'shrub', which is also the Hindi word for alcoholic drink.

# frozen strawberry
# daiquiri

Daiquiris always look so festive, and you can change the fruit to taste: pineapple or banana are both great! I like to use golden rum because it has a better taste, but the colour will change somewhat.

*juice of 2 limes*

*2 tablespoons icing sugar*

*125 ml white rum*

*6 strawberries*

*dash of strawberry liqueur (optional)*

*about 250 ml crushed ice*

**SERVES 2**

Put all the ingredients into a blender and blend until frothy. Pour into chilled daiquiri glasses – preferably enormous!

# daiquiri
# granita

Put 25 ml sugar syrup and 75 ml lime juice into a blender, add 350 ml rum, a dash of grenadine and 250 ml ice, blend until frothy and serve in chilled glasses. (Sugar syrup is 2–3 parts water, 1 part sugar, boiled for 2 minutes, then cooled).

**Serves 2**

# lemon-bacardi
# daiquiri

Put 3 parts Bacardi into a blender, add 2 parts lemon juice, 1 part sugar syrup and 250 ml crushed ice. Blend until frothy, then serve in chilled glasses.

**Serves 4–5**

# mint mojito

The Caribbean and Central America have created some fabulous taste combinations, often based on rum.

A mojito is essentially a rum julep, and you can make it in the same way as the Mint Julep on page 116. However, being lazy, I like mine made in a blender, and just love the amazing colour produced by the blended mint leaves.

Traditional recipes use soda water as a top-up, but I prefer sparkling mineral water. This is also great without the rum (and without the top-up mixer), but, either way, it's a perfect summer cooler!

*125 ml white rum*
*juice of 1 large lime*
*4 tablespoons icing sugar, or to taste*
*ice cubes*
*soda water or sparkling mineral water*

**to serve**
*leaves from a large bunch of mint, plus extra sprigs*
*a curl of lime zest*
**SERVES 1**

Put the rum into a blender, add the lime juice, sugar, 4 ice cubes, 125 ml sparkling mineral water and the mint leaves and blend until bright green. Strain through a fine sieve into a jug, then pour into a tall glass packed with ice. Top with mineral water or soda water to taste, add the curl of lime zest and a sprig of mint and serve.

To serve a larger number of people, increase the quantities accordingly, and, instead of pouring into glasses, pour into a jug one-third full of ice, then top with mineral water and serve.

Caribbean mojitos are the coolest of all rum drinks – and I also like them made with tequila. Before serving, strain this drink through a fine-mesh sieve to remove the pieces of chopped mint, leaving the liquid a bright, clear, beautiful green.

# whisky
## mac

Utterly delicious for people who like their drinks spicy, but not too sweet. For a weaker version, serve in a long glass and top up with a soft drink.

*1 measure whisky*
*1 measure green ginger wine*
*ice*

**to serve**
*a curl of lemon peel*
*ginger ale or ginger beer (optional)*
**SERVES 1**

Put the whisky and ginger wine into a cocktail shaker filled with ice. Shake well, then strain into a small glass and serve with a curl of lemon peel. For a longer drink, top up with ginger ale or ginger beer, if using.

# whisky
## sour

I like my sours properly sour, but if you're less adventurous, add a teaspoon of sugar syrup.

*35 ml bourbon or whisky*
*the juice of ½ lemon*
**SERVES 1**

Put the bourbon or whisky into a cocktail shaker filled with ice, shake well, then strain into a whisky sour glass.

## kumquat
# ratafia

Kumquats in brandy were a great tradition when I was growing up – no-one could think of anything else to do with the tiny, bitter, jewel-like oranges. Much too strong for children of course, but the adults seemed to love them (I found out why when I grew up).

*kumquats, about 1–2 punnets (see method)*
*sugar (see method)*
*1 cinnamon stick*
*3 cloves*
*brandy (see method)*

*1-litre preserving jar*
**MAKES 1 JAR, ABOUT 1 LITRE**

Wash the kumquats and prick them several times with a skewer or needle. Pack them into the preserving jar and fit crossed bamboo skewers over the top to keep the fruit from rising in the liquid. Fill the jar one-third full with sugar, add the cinnamon and cloves, top up with brandy and set aside for about 2 months.

Serve the liquid as in the previous recipe. The fruit is wonderful sliced and served in fruit puddings, or pan-fried in butter and served with meat or game

## spiced orange
# ratafia

*grated zest and juice of 6 large oranges*
*500 g sugar*
*1 cinnamon stick*
*½ teaspoon ground coriander*
*1.25 litres brandy*

*2-litre preserving jar*
**MAKES 1 JAR, ABOUT 2 LITRES**

Put the zest and juice into the preserving jar. Add the sugar, cinnamon stick and ground coriander.

Stir until the sugar has dissolved and let stand for about 30–60 minutes. Pour over 1.25 litres brandy, cover with a lid and shake the jar. Set aside for 2 months, shaking the jar from time to time. Serve as a liqueur, poured over ice or as a long drink with a mixer. I also like this as a sauce for ice cream, sometimes with a light extra sprinkling of finely grated orange zest.

Ratafias are simple to make – just fresh ripe fruits macerated in brandy.

# mint julep

Traditionally, a mint julep should be served in a silver or pewter mug, so the frosty surface isn't marred by finger marks, but a chilled glass jug, tall, frosty glasses and a drinking straw work just as well.

*6 tablespoons sugar syrup*

*24–30 mint leaves, torn, plus sprigs of mint*

*1 teaspoon Angostura Bitters (optional)*

*375 ml bourbon*

*ice cubes*

**SERVES 4**

Muddle the sugar syrup in a jug with the mint leaves and Bitters, if using. Alternatively, use a mortar and pestle. Stir in the bourbon. Pack a chilled jug with ice and mint sprigs, then strain in the julep.

Alternatively, pack tall glasses with ice, then pour over the julep. Serve with straws.

**VARIATION** *BRANDY MINT JULEP*

Use brandy instead of bourbon and serve as in the main recipe.

# mango
## and ginger
# kir royale

Kir Royale is cassis with champagne. This party drink is based on that idea, and, if you serve it, you won't have to worry about providing anything else. For my mango and ginger version, I use canned Indian Alphonso mango purée when I'm outside mango growing country, and huge ripe Bowen mangoes from Queensland when I'm in Australia. You can also use frozen mango, blended while still frozen to an icy purée. If using fresh or frozen mangoes, you'll have to add a little lemon juice to develop the flavour and ice to help smash the fibre.

1 jar preserved stem ginger, pieces cut into
    quarters, or crystallized ginger
500 ml mango purée
8 tablespoons ginger purée or juice*
syrup from the jar of stem ginger (optional)
sugar, to taste
6 bottles chilled champagne (8 glasses per bottle
    for champagne cocktails)

**MAKES AT LEAST 50 GLASSES**

Thread the quarter pieces of ginger, lengthways, onto the end of a long cocktail stick or bamboo skewer. Arrange them on a plate or in a bowl, ginger ends downward.

Working in batches if necessary, put the mango purée into a blender, add the ginger purée or juice, the syrup from the jar, if using, and 250 ml iced water. Blend well.

Add sugar to taste. Blend again, then add more iced water until the mixture is the texture of thin cream – if it's too thick it will fall to the bottom of the glass.

Arrange champagne flutes on serving trays, then put 1 teaspoon of the mango mixture into each one. Add a small teaspoon of champagne, stir and set aside until your guests arrive. When they do, top up the glasses with champagne (twice, because they bubble like mad), then put a ginger cocktail stick across the top of each one and tell your guests it's a swizzle stick. They will want more, so have extra mango mixture ready.

*****Note**  Ginger purée is sold in jars in some supermarkets. To make your own, cut 1 kg fresh ginger into pieces about 5 cm long. Soak in water to cover for about 30 minutes, then peel and chop coarsely. Transfer to a blender or spice grinder and work to a purée. You may need to add a little iced water. You can press the juice through a strainer or freeze the pulp in ice cube trays, then use in this and other recipes as needed. You'll need at least 8 cubes for this recipe.

# rosa-
# frizzare

A refreshing combination from Southern Italy. Mix 100 ml Campari and 400 ml grapefruit juice in a jug. To serve, half-fill each glass with the mixture, add ice and top up with champagne. For a special party, decorate with sprigs of mint.

**Serves 6**

# mandarin
# fizz

Mix 1 litre mandarin juice and 250 ml Cointreau or Grand Marnier in a chilled jug.

To serve, pour a little of the mixture into each glass, then top with champagne.

For a single cocktail, omit the champagne and pour the fiery juice over ice.

**Serves 12–16**

# bellini
# kir

Put about 2 tablespoons peach liqueur and some sliced peach into each champagne glass and top with iced champagne or other sparkling wine.

**Serves 1 or many**

I created the Mango and Ginger Kir Royale (a South-east Asian version of a traditional Provençal Kir Royale) to serve at a book launch. I knew I was onto a winner when we just couldn't keep up with the demand. Try it at your next party.

# champagne
## cocktail

This delicious champagne cocktail is also a variation on the popular Kir Royale.

*1 teaspoon of a liqueur such as Poire William, peach or strawberry liqueur, framboise, Midori, blue curaçao or Galliano (if using Galliano, add the pulp and seeds of 1 passionfruit)*
*alternatively, 4 tablespoons fruit juice, such as pear, pineapple, peach or apricot*
*1 shot of vodka (optional)*
*champagne or other sparkling wine*
**SERVES 1**

Put 1 teaspoon of liqueur or 4 tablespoons fruit juice into a champagne flute or coupé, add the vodka, if using, and top up with champagne.

For extra pizzazz, decorate the glass with a fine slice of the fruit used to make the liqueur.

# blue
## champagne

Spectacularly chic, this is one you should only serve if you're prepared for your guests to be merry in a matter of seconds. Serve to the firstcomers – otherwise everyone will want one!

*2 teaspoons freshly squeezed lemon juice*
*½ teaspoon Triple Sec or Cointreau**
*½ teaspoon blue curaçao*
*125 ml vodka*
*champagne or other sparkling wine*
**SERVES 2**

Put ice cubes into a cocktail shaker, then add the lemon juice, Triple Sec or Cointreau, curaçao and vodka.

Shake, then strain into 2 champagne flutes and top up with champagne.

***Note** Triple Sec is best, but can be difficult to find. Use any dry orange-flavoured liqueur instead – Cointreau is the most common.

Champagne is the great party drink and champagne cocktails are equally popular: make them with fruit purées, added spirits or liqueurs – all delicious.

This traditional English summertime drink is perfect for tennis parties and polo matches. When the borage herb is in flower, freeze the pretty blue blossoms in ice cubes for out-of-season drinks.

## pimms

Allow 250 ml per drink, and at least 2 drinks per person if serving Pimms for a party and be prepared for repeat orders! The cucumber is mandatory – somehow it wouldn't be Pimms without it. Look out for the small Lebanese cucumbers shown on this page – you can cut them lengthways to make pretty shapes. Take care – this delicious cooler tastes heavenly, but is deceptively strong.

*1 part Pimms*
*3 parts ginger ale, lemonade or soda*
*borage flowers*
*curls of cucumber peel*
*sliced lemons and sprigs of mint*
**SERVES 1 OR A PARTY**

Put all the ingredients into a jug of ice and serve.

# ruby grapefruit campari

Wonderful for a summer party – serve one tall glass per person as a welcoming drink. Campari at this level of dilution isn't very intoxicating, so this is a perfect drink for early in the day and absolutely gorgeous for brunch parties.

*1 litre ruby grapefruit juice, chilled*

*125 ml Campari, or to taste*

*250 ml crushed ice*

*sprigs of mint, to serve*

**SERVES 8–10**

Put the grapefruit juice, Campari and crushed ice into a blender and blend briefly.

Half-fill a jug with more crushed ice and cram lots of mint sprigs into the jug. Pour the Campari mixture over the top, then serve.

# index

## picture credits and acknowledgements

William Lingwood (from *Fingerfood, Juices and Tonics* and *A Handful of Herbs*)
p. 3–5, p. 9, p. 12–13, p. 18–19, p. 22–25, p. 30–31, p. 36–37, p. 42–44, p.46–47, p. 50–51, p. 54–59, p. 61–74, p. 76–77, p. 80–81, p.83, p. 86–87, p. 90–94, p. 100–103, p. 110–111, p. 115, p. 118–122

James Merrell (from *Coolers and Summer Cocktails* and *Smoothies and Other Blended Drinks*) p. 1–2, p. 6–7, p. 15, p. 21, p. 27–28, p. 33–35, p. 38–40, p. 45, p. 48, p. 52–53, p. 60, p. 75, p. 78, p. 82, p. 84, p. 88–89, p. 95–96, p. 99, p. 104–109, p. 112–114, p. 116–117, p. 123–125, p.128

Debi Treloar (from *Smoothies and Shakes* and *Soda Fountain Classics*) p. 11, p. 16–17, p. 41

Pia Tryde (from *Pure Style Outside*) p. 98

Christopher Drake (from *Open Air Living*) p. 20, p. 97